Ghosts of Christchurch Hundred

Michael A. Hodges

ISBN 1 897 887 31 0

A British Library Cataloguing in Publication data. A catalogue record for this book is available from the British Library.

Published by: Natula Publications
5 St Margaret's Avenue, Christchurch, Dorset, BH23 1JD.
www.natula.co.uk

The Publisher is grateful to the Red House Museum for permission to use their illustrations reproduced on the following pages: -

9,17,18,20,21,22,25,26,28,30,31,33,35,36,52,55,60.

Front cover illustration: Aerial Photograph of Christchurch
Back cover illustration: Invalids Walk, Bournemouth

CONTENTS

ILLUSTRATIONS

What is a Ghost?

There is no definitive view as to what is a ghost. There is a widespread, but not a universal view that whatever it is that we call a ghost can exist. Generally thought of as a 'spirit' and often concerning a deceased living thing, our perception of what we may label as ghostly depends at any particular time upon one or more of our senses: sight, sound, smell, touch, taste and psi. The latter, sixth sense, which has only recently been recognised, is associated with telepathy, precognition and other aspects of the mind.

There are many possibilities of what ghosts are including: reflections of strong emotional experiences that have become imprinted on a place or object; spirits of the dead who still have some sort of self aware existence and can react to the living, or shades of the dead which replay certain appearances like a film show but without self knowledge. Ghosts can also be spirits of the dead who are aware of their situation as dead, or entities, or energies which seek to influence physical events though the living. They can be discarnate entities of non-human origin or energies released by persons undergoing puberty or another intense undirected sexual power. They can also be energies released by building or other work disturbing the structure of a place where emotional events have occurred. Ghosts can be creations within the human mind, particularly when the individual is tired, or under stress, or influenced by drugs, or preconditioned to expect an experience.

Out of body and near death experiences would seem to indicate that the human mind and personality could survive the loss of function of the human body.

It has also been suggested that ghosts occur as examples of time slip. Since time is only a human perception and does not really exist as a one directional river, in which the human brain sees past, present and future separately. Hence everything occurs as in a book and our perception of time is based on our view from the page we are on and sometimes another page is glimpsed. Time itself is relative to location and velocity in space and ourselves as observers.

Another view of time is that there are multi-universes in parallel and people may get views and events in different universes, so accounting for the appearance of living persons as ghosts, or for an individual seeing themselves – doppelganger.

Perhaps ghosts can be any or all of these things.

People near to the 'presence' of a ghost frequently mention a drop in temperature. This is likely to be the result of energy being taken up to power the manifestation. This coldness is noticeable in a number of cases reported in this book. Similarly electrical interference is also frequently associated with ghosts, for example lights turning on and off or equipment ceasing to function. Such happenings may also be electromagnetic effects of energy being sought.

Where to Find a Ghost

If ghosts are linked to emotion and/or to feelings of stress then we should expect to find them at places where feelings can be strong, e.g. churches, monasteries, hospitals, orphanages, workhouses, prisons or barracks. Such places may be sites where people have experienced: relief, fear, joy, sadness, pain, death or sexual frustration. These feelings may leave a mark that other people can instinctively feel. It is noticeable that monastery sites that comprise what was once a mixture of a church, hospital, hotel, school, prison and barracks are well provided with ghostly happenings. Those nearest to Christchurch were at Wimborne, Breamore and Beaulieu, and all have tales of phantoms.

Concentration of strong feelings may also arise at inns and hotels were people have said farewell to loved ones travelling to distant lands, or where the availability of alcohol has encouraged violent acts, or where opportunities for sexual activity have been widely indulged – guilty pleasures of brothels. Certainly inns feature widely at locations were ghosts are reported. Of course this may be due to stories being made up to entertain and to give local colour to the pub.

Other false ghost stories may have arisen due to smuggling, once the main industry of the Christchurch area. Smugglers did not want witnesses, nor did they want people to investigate locations where they hid their goods. Hence ghost stories could be invented and told to deter the curious from visiting certain places. Groups of armed men operating at night created a threatening environment, and the use of spout lanterns to call in vessels "on (to) the spot" to land cargoes, and the use of flints to "flash off" vessels when the revenue were about, all added to the atmosphere of mystery. Similarly tales of large, ferocious animals roaming the countryside after dark, such as the black dog of Portland, would be told as a deterrent to keep people indoors at night. The availability of cheap spirits probably encouraged exaggerated story telling.

Ghosts are often reported at night when a place is quiet, without activity or movement and light. Hence, there is an absence of distractions to disturb the mind of an observer. There are probably many ghost stories that are never reported because people are embarrassed and afraid of being subjects for laughter or thought to be odd. It is hoped that this book will encourage more people to come forward and share their experiences. Most people believe in ghosts, whatever they may be, but many people do not volunteer having seen one. If ghosts do exist, other than in the mind, then they are a natural phenomena and worthy of study.

Christchurch Priory and Graveyard

Christchurch Hundred

Christchurch is an ancient borough, once a Saxon burgh (fort) on the coast east of Bournemouth at the southwest edge of the New Forest. It was a Saxon Hundred, so called because land was divided as units of 100 farms for taxation and law and order. Each farm was known as a hide, a ploughland, which could support a warrior, his weapons (spear and shield) and his family. The Burgh (borough) of Christchurch required 470 warriors for its defence; it provided a refuge for an area of about a 20-mile radius. The adjacent burghs were Southampton, Wareham and Wilton. At the time of the Normans' arrival in England Christchurch was only one of three boroughs in Hampshire, the other two were Winchester and Southampton, and so Christchurch was an important place.

Christchurch Castle Keep Ruins

The Normans called it the Hundred of Edgegate because it was at the edge of the New Forest. The Saxons had known it as Tweoxneam, the place betwixt the waters. This was because the town itself is situated at the confluence of the Avon and the Stour at the head of the harbour, which emerges at The Run, Mudeford, into Christchurch Bay, with the Isle of Wight to the southeast and the Isle of Purbeck to the southwest.

The River Avon gave access to Wiltshire and Salisbury Plain; the River Stour provided a route into Dorset via Blandford and to Cranborne Chase by means of the River Allen at Wimborne. The Avon was once an approximate boundary between Celtic Arthurian Britons to the west and Saxon England to the east. The Saxon Kingdom of Wessex then absorbed the whole area, but now a boundary again exists with Hampshire in the South East Region of England and Dorset in the South West.

In addition to the land comprising the current Borough of Christchurch, Christchurch Hundred included areas roughly described by the parishes of Sopley, Milton, Milford and Hordle; part of the New Forest as far east as Boldre and the tithings west of the River Stour, now Bournemouth – Muscliff, Muccleshell, Throop, Holdenhurst, Iford and Tuckton (the Liberty of Westover). At one time the town of Lymington was also included in Christchurch Hundred.

William The Conqueror created the New Forest as a royal hunting preserve in about 1074. Many of the English Kings shared the Conqueror's love of hunting and the hunting lodges in the New Forest may have been convenient places to escape from the public life of the Court. The forest also provided training for war and horse management. New Forest laws imposed cruel punishments like blinding and castration for killing the King's beasts – deer and wild boar, whereas Saxon hunting laws had only imposed fines.

Despite the rich history of the area ghosts from more than ten generations in the past (about 300 years) seem to be rare. Prehistoric, Celtic, Roman, Saxon, Viking or Norman ghosts do not appear as frequently as the long association of such people within the area would seem to warrant. So perhaps ghosts have a limited life. Maybe the energies required to reveal them disperse over time so that they slowly become more difficult to perceive.

Christchurch Quay, Place Mill and Priory

The Great Quire, Christchurch Priory

Reported Hauntings

Christchurch Priory

The great Augustinian Priory, on the site of a Saxon Minster, around which the town of Christchurch has developed, contained many holy relics and treasures and was an important place of pilgrimage in medieval times. In 1539 when Henry VIII suppressed the Priory, ordering its sale and the removal of all its treasures, he was persuaded to return the church to the people of Christchurch for use as their parish church.

Different people have reported seeing ghostly visions at various parts of Christchurch Priory on many occasions. The figure of a monk, thought to be John Draper, the last Prior who died in 1552, has been spotted on several occasions at the entrance to the Draper Chapel, which is next to the foot of the Southern Stair Tower. He was buried in the Nave in front of the altar but his grave slab has been moved. A figure in Augustinian attire was once seen entering the Chapel by a young woman but not by another person who was standing in front of the Chapel. He was adamant that the Chapel was empty. So it appears that ghosts are only visible to certain people or perhaps to people only at a certain distance.

On another occasion a clergyman was showing his son around the Priory when the youth asked how it was that the church still had monks. The young man had seen a figure in a monk's robe on the left in the Great Quire when looking from the Nave.

A medium once claimed to have made contact with Prior Draper and also with the Prior's cook and that they revealed that holy relics and treasure were hidden in the Priory. Such treasures were thought to include silver and gilt covered wooden statues of saints, the empty niches for which can be seen in the Jessie Screen at the Great Quire.

The Draper Chapel, Christchurch Priory

The medium claimed that the cache was in a grave originally for Christopher Stenhouse but now with the slab reversed and bearing another name. Many graves may have contained lead coffins and such coffins were melted down to make shot during the Civil War. (See the tomb of Henry Rogers in the churchyard, which may have been used for the bones of monks whose coffins were melted down.)

A former vicar, on his way home to the vicarage late one night, decided to take a short cut through the church. Here he witnessed a ghostly funeral procession of monks taking a coffin from the Priory to the monks graveyard on the south side of the church.

One evening in the 1970's a couple doing the church accounts in the vestry had locked the doors in the Priory for security. They heard loud footsteps from the Quire Aisle, which sounded like wooden soled sandals on a stone floor, but the Quire Aisle is carpeted. When they went to look no one was there.

On occasions the sound of chanting has been reported from the Priory when no service or concert was being held.

In the 1970's there were also reports of frankincense in use at the Priory. The author challenged the then vicar when he smelt incense on the north side of the altar in the Nave. The vicar remarked that two other people had mentioned it but on the south side of the altar, but that the Church of England had not used incense in the Priory since 1539. Different people have smelt incense subsequently; many reports during the 1990's mention noticing it around the South Nave Aisle, the smell getting stronger nearer to the Prior's Door. Perhaps the scent relates to a ghostly procession.

There have been reports of strange events happening in St. Michael's Loft, above the east end of the Priory, and in the stair towers. Some seventy years ago one person made a sworn statement as to what they had experienced. "On the 11th October at about 3.30pm I had an occasion to ascend the staircase (from the South Quire Aisle) leading to St. Michael's Loft. When I reached the staircase the top of the first flight of steps and halfway up the next flight, something seemed to push past me and I felt as if I was not alone, but I saw nothing. I stopped as the occurrence gave me a turn. I then proceeded up the steps and within site of the open doorway of St. Michael's Loft I saw a figure standing in the doorway. It was the figure of a human being but appeared to be transparent, arms held by its side, I did not know whether draped or not. I stopped again for I felt a considerable shock. The figure still being in the doorway, I approached to the door so that I might perform the work I had come to do, and the figure retreated to towards the schoolmaster's desk at the end (of the room) and then vanished. I saw nothing on my return journey. On giving up the key at the west end (of the Nave) I sat down for a few minutes as I felt shaken".

On more recent occasions persons using St. Michael's Loft have reported the sensation of someone or something brushing past them on to the Stair Tower Steps.

In 1999 a case of automatic writing occurred in St. Michael's Loft (once a boys Grammar School and now a museum). A Priory official was alone on duty in the museum and seated at a table looking towards the mannequin display of a figure in the attire of an Augustinian monk. The official heard a loud crash above his head and then began to write automatically in archaic French. When translated the writing was found to refer to a monk named Stephen son of Richard de Montreuil, who died aged 60 in 1345 at the Priory. It is possible that Stephen was from Stalbridge in north Dorset and had been with the Templars when they were disbanded in 1311. Templecombe near Stalbridge was a Templar site. Because of his association with that Order he was persecuted. He escaped from custody but was recaptured and was sentenced to be a perpetual novice monk at Christchurch. The night after this experience the Priory official (Archivist) had a dream in which he learned that Stephen's mother was Angelique de Tournai. In 2000 the Priory sold unwanted stone to a local architectural antiques yard. Amongst the stone was a large grave slab, broken into three, which bore the symbol of a large two-handed sword with fleur de lys, one on the pommel, one on the blade and one at the end of each quillon. It is remotely possible that the sword (not a Templar type) was a memorial for Stephen's life as a Templar. Alternatively it could be for Walter de Pinkney who predeceased him by about 200 years.

Repairs were being made to a Norman arch at the Priory in June 1972. During this time the peace was occasionally disturbed by the noise of a phantom mason working. This was often at weekends when no work was actually in progress and the workmen were not even on site. It seems as if the disturbance of the work done some 900 years previously had triggered some echoes.

Stone Coffin with skeleton found in the monastic precinct

Priory House, built for Gustavus Brander in 1777, is only about a fathom from the south side of the Priory. This building, which is in the monastic precinct, also has ghostly experiences. When it was still in use as a home a young expectant mother was in bed when all the covers were violently pulled off the bed while she lay in it.

The Priory Cottage, the former Porter's Lodge at the entrance to the monastery (now at the entrance to the Priory car park) also has a ghost, 'Old Joe', who apparently was once a verger at the Priory. His figure was seen on various occasions in the early 1950's standing on the raised garden area near the cottage, which is visible from Quay Road.

Church Street, Castle Street & Bridge Street

Christchurch Castle was a Norman motte and bailey castle with a stone Constable's Hall and keep. Several monarchs visited the castle from William the Conqueror onwards. Situated behind the properties at the junction of Church Street and Castle Street the castle is now a ruin having been slighted by Parliamentarian forces after the Civil War.

Church St, Castle St and Christchurch Castle

In the 1980's a new pub The Castle Tavern was created in the premises of a former tearooms in Church Street. When the alterations were in progress a tiler working in the ground floor kitchen found the atmosphere such that he could not work alone there in the evenings. Soon after opening a misty shape was seen emerging from the wall near a fireplace inside the pub. The shape disappeared gradually down through the floor, apparently following the slope of the Castle ditch around the Norman motte, now covered by the buildings on the east side of Church Street. An atmosphere had also been noticed in the first floor kitchen and glasses seemed to move off shelves and fall. Other reported sightings included the figure of an old lady on the stairs; a man in black sitting at a table at the back of the pub; a small boy who came up to the table smiling. These last two figures were seen out of the corner of an eye, but when looked at directly they disappeared.

The Castle Tavern has recently been refurbished and extensively modernised into a light and airy bar, now renamed as the Soho Bar – possibly less conducive for seeing ghosts?

Ye Olde George Inn, formerly St. George and The Dragon, in Castle Street, is the oldest pub in Christchurch, and was once a coaching inn. Like so many old places in the town, it was used by smugglers. The buildings, dating from the 14th century and containing a priest's hole are supposed to be haunted by a female ghost known as the Grey Lady. Regulars have allegedly seen her throw condiments off the pub tables.

A figure of Civil War solider, in armour, with his horse has been seen in a **Bridge Street** back garden, possibly that of Quartley's or Tyneham House. Christchurch Castle stood a three-day close siege in January 1645. Cannon balls have been found in the Mill Stream and body and armour parts in the River Avon by Town Bridge and also in the Mill Stream nearby.

The sound of pilgrims singing and chanting to pipes and drums has been heard from **Town Bridge**. Pilgrims were attracted to the Priory due to relics of Thomas à Becket. Pilgrims also visited Beaulieu Abbey locally. Other pilgrim routes were Salisbury to Glastonbury, Winchester to Canterbury and Poole to Santiago (Spain) at a reported cost of 7/6d (37½ p) for a single fare. The travellers were advised to bring their own food and bedding and take their chance with Moorish slavers.

Town Bridge, Bridge Street and the River Avon

High Street, Wick Lane, Quay Road and Sopers Lane

The Regent Centre, built in the High Street in 1931 as a cinema, is now also a theatre and concert hall and has two ghosts. In about 1986 a couple were seen in the front stalls at the right hand side. Also noises had been heard in the room behind the stage and objects moved. There had been reports that the changing room above the studio at the rear end of the building had an oppressive atmosphere and patches of coldness at times. Much renovation work has been carried out at the Regent Centre recently with the room behind the stage being demolished and rebuilt. There have been no recent reports of ghostly activity.

In the 1980's staff at **Woolworths,** near the Regent Centre in the High Street, reported seeing figures walking through walls and hearing strange noises. In late 2001 similar reports were made involving figures, noises and lights going on or off in the evening when the store was closed.

Christchurch High Street
(with the Regent Centre, Woolworths and the Corn Factors)

Behind Woolworths was a former **Corn Factors building.** For many years it was derelict but faces were seen at its windows when it was known to be empty and its doors were locked. The building has now been demolished.

The Library in the High Street was once the home of the Druitt family. In 1943, the year that Herbert Druitt died, an apparition of a lady in grey was seen walking down the stairs. It is assumed that this was the ghost of Herbert's mother Matilda.

The Thomas Tripp, formerly The Plumber's Arms, Wick Lane, is said to be haunted by John Lovell according to the present landlord, his son, John. John Lovell (Senior) was also at different times the licensee of the Olde George and The Ship Inns in Christchurch.

The Red House Museum in Quay Road was originally the Christchurch Workhouse.

The Red House Museum, formerly a workhouse

A former member of staff believed the building to be haunted by various figures and reported hearing strange noises. As a workhouse it would have seen much misery. Later the building belonged to the Druitt family and Herbert used it for his extensive collection of antiquities. The Druitts were important people in Christchurch and originally haled from Wimborne. It has been suggested that Montague Druitt, son of a surgeon at Wimborne, was Jack the Ripper. His mother died insane and he committed suicide, after which the Ripper murders in London ceased.

Place Mill, a site mentioned in the Domesday Book, was used for centuries to grind corn for the town and was also the haunt of smugglers. Its working life stopped at the beginning of the 20th century when structural defects forced it to close. 'Shapes' have been seen on the first floor in the grain hopper.

Sopers Lane is an ancient route from Pound Lane and Bargates to the Wick Ferry; a road probably used by characters like Sam Hookey, 'the wicked man of Wick', a smuggler who was also a blacksmith at Pound Lane. In 1998 the lady of a house adjoining Sopers Lane saw, inside her house, in daylight, a male figure with white whiskers. She then realised she could see through the figure and that it was not her husband who was upstairs.

Bargates and the Barrack Road

At **Christchurch Conservative Club** in the Assembly Rooms on the first floor footsteps have been heard when the Rooms were empty. A female figure dressed in brown has been seen on the stairs going from the ground floor toilets up to the Assembly Rooms when they were not being used and the steward's second floor flat was unoccupied.

The Fusee, Bargates, is now an office but originally was built as a fusee chain factory, where the employees were mainly women and children. Footsteps have been heard crossing the first floor at about 10-11pm at night when no one was upstairs.

Royalty Inn, formerly the Red Lion, is situated on land that once belonged to St Mary Magdalene's Lazar House (medieval hospital). A figure has been seen and objects have moved and doors have closed of their own accord.

In 1987 the lady owner of a house in **Avon Buildings**, off Bargates and close to the River Avon, was sitting in her ground floor lounge doing some embroidery when she became aware of someone standing next to her. It was a male figure of medium height, with short grey curly hair and beard, wearing a coarsely woven brown robe with no hood and a rope girdle – similar to those worn by lay canons or friars. His expression was gentle and the atmosphere peaceful. When she spoke to him, the figure disappeared. A year or so later the same figure appeared in the doorway of the same room. When she looked at him directly the figure vanished.

Stour Cottage, the building housing the amusement arcade in Barrack Road alongside the recreation ground, has had reports of amusement machines being moved about when no one was there.

The Bailey Bridge Hotel, Barrack Road, next to the Bailey Bridge Inn has been built on the site of a sports field – empty land belonging to the former Christchurch Barracks, (The Bailey Bridge was invented at Christchurch Barracks). Two of the hotel bedrooms, one above the other, have had objects moved, doors opening and things occurring for no apparent reason. A strange atmosphere has been felt by cleaners; one lady felt a hand on her shoulder. Also table settings have been disturbed and cutlery found on the floor.

Stour Cottage, Barrack Road

Stable and Barrack Block, Christchurch Barracks, is now flats. The site was a barracks from 1794 to 1994; it was used by cavalry, RHA, RA and Royal Engineers. About 1972 at 2 am one morning a security man was on patrol on the back stairs of the old barrack block. He had inspected the small room containing a safe and began to walk along the first floor corridor. He noticed a light behind him and turned around. There was the figure of a First World War soldier, wearing boots, puttees, khaki trousers, white shirt and peaked cap. He was smoking a cigarette. The security man asked 'Who are you?' The ghost stared at him, smoke curling from the cigarette, then the figure slowly disappeared like the smoke. The security man was so shaken that he resigned his job the same day. It appears that there had been a suicide by a soldier held in detention in the Barracks during the First World War.

Christchurch Barracks, 1794 - 1994

In 1980 another security man, an ex-school head teacher between teaching jobs, was employed at the Barracks. He knew nothing of the ghost since the security man from the story above had only told his superior when resigning.

The former teacher was in the same corridor having checked the safe. He too was surprised to see a soldier in similar clothing, although he described a white vest and broad braces but no cigarette. The ghost and he looked at each other and then the security man ran down the stairs. He refused to return to the building and resigned the same week.

Our informant, the security supervisor, reported an experience in the same corridor. He saw nothing but felt on one occasion as if he had walked into a refrigerator and hurried away from the place. A member of staff who often worked long hours in the building never reported any untoward experience, but he never ventured upstairs. This is perhaps another example of ghosts only appearing to certain people or only on certain occasions.

Fairmile

The area beneath the **Railway Bridge over the River Avon** is said to have an unhappy atmosphere. It is the approximate location of where in 1935 Mrs Rattenbury, a Bournemouth resident, committed suicide after the murder of her husband. George Stoner, her lover, was found guilty during the trial at the Old Bailey but Mrs Rattenbury was completely absolved of the murder charge. A week later, having found a peaceful spot on the riverbank, she stabbed herself 5 times and threw herself into the river.

Christchurch Hospital was formerly a workhouse serving Christchurch and Bournemouth. The Board Room, now unfortunately destroyed by fire, in Jumpers Road was supposed to be haunted.

Part of Bronte and Emily Avenues are on the site of **Cottage Homes**, the former children's orphanage. Children's footsteps and the sound of children's voices playing can be heard upstairs in houses which are empty, or outside in the early hours of the morning.

Somerford and Purewell

A local newspaper reports that in October 1972, the inhabitants of a house in **Amethyst Road,** Somerford, were disturbed by loud knocking on their doors and windows. Whenever they investigated there was no one there. They tried various ways to identify the culprits such as sprinkling flour around outside to obtain their footprints but the flour remained undisturbed. The 'Knocker' was only active in the evening and during the months from September to March. The married daughter of the occupants had had a similar experience at South Bockhampton, Bransgore.

Somerford, with Amethyst Road (centre)

Somerford Road, at its eastern end, is near to site of Somerford Grange, the retirement home of Prior Draper and the former farm of Christchurch Monastery. A hooded figure, probably a monk wearing a cowel, was seen on the road and caused car drivers to swerve or stop. This was reported by a former mayor's chauffeur in the 1970's when he stopped the car thinking he had run a figure over. Another ex-mayor who swerved to avoid a hooded figure told a similar story. His car struck the opposite pavement shaking him up. On a different occasion a lady driving from Christchurch who thought she had run into a figure at the same location reported a similar event. As in so many cases, these three people kept their story to themselves for years for fear of being mocked.

A member of a congregation at a church in the **Purewell** area was told by her priest about "grey matter" which would surround the altar area. He told her it was accompanied by giving him feelings of depression.

The **Salisbury Arms** in Purewell only became licensed premises in about 1878. Before that time it had been 2 cottages with a brew house behind them. A few years ago the cleaner at the pub reported seeing a man in a blue frock coat standing in the bar (in the area that would have been the yard behind the cottages) watching her. The children of a previous manager have also seen this figure upstairs at night. Other ghostly occurrences include light bulbs and their shades descending from the ceiling, just missing customers, on many occasions; alarms have been activated for no apparent reason and customers at the bar have been aware of a dog brushing past them when there was no animal around at all.

Highcliffe

The 1832 mansion known as **Highcliffe Castle** was once used to entertain British and European royalty, aristocracy and politicians. In the 1990's the 'Castle' underwent major restoration following its destruction from fires and vandalism. As a result parts of the building are now open to the public. The Council's Manager of the Castle took a flash photograph in the former Library for the first exhibition. As he did so the door slammed shut, the conservatory doors opened and he heard footsteps on the gravel outside – but no one was there. Lights in a display case came on again after being switched off.

Violet Stuart Wortley, who lived at Highcliffe Castle at the turn of the last century, believed it to be full of ghosts and wrote as such in her letters. However, she did not seem at all perturbed by them. These earlier stories about ghostly events at the building concern doors opening when they were tight shut; maidservants in upstairs bedrooms were disturbed and sought to move to other parts of the house because they were frightened, and a figure of a woman was seen looking out from a window in the West Tower. There have also been reports of a presence felt in the Library.

Highcliffe Castle Library, with Conservatory beyond

The Claretian Missionary Fathers reported similar experiences in the 1950's – 60's. One priest jammed the Library door open with a wooden chock, but the door slammed shut and the wood chock flew across the room.

Practitioners of Wicca, a Pagan religion invented by Gerald Gardner when he was a resident at Highcliffe have used Chewton Common, which is nearby. It has also been suggested that last century a coven of witches met at a house in this area, possibly Mill House.

The **Mill House** in Chewton, Highcliffe, is situated on the bank of the Chewton Bunny in a secluded area surrounded by trees and set back from the road. The building dates from the 18th century but was built on the site of an old mill that was mentioned in ancient charters of Christchurch Priory. The Chewton Bunny was a route used by smugglers from the shore travelling inland to the Cat and Fiddle and deep into the New Forest. It is conceivable that Mill House was used as a hiding place for their contraband. A figure of a young man has been seen in a room here dressed in early 20th century clothing, but no one was actually there.

Mill House, Chewton

In 1940 a cone of power was raised by witches at **Highcliffe Beach** to resist the threatened German Invasion.

New Forest - Southern Area

The Old Vicarage, Hinton Admiral, situated at the junction of Station Road and Lyndhurst Road is now a hotel. The Magnolia Room (since renamed) is an upstairs bedroom that can go icy cold. Female staff have felt a presence there and a smell of flowers has been noticed. A dog once reacted badly in this room. A former owner reported that the mirror has shown what appeared to be London Bridge in its reflection. In the hotel lights have gone dim and turned on and off. An electrician called in to do some work left hurriedly when he found no light bulb in a room that had nevertheless been illuminated. In the bar footsteps can be clearly heard from the room above even when it is empty.

Shortly after the new owners moved in the back door swung open and the cellar door crashed open loudly in the opposite direction. Jokingly the chef said it must be a ghost and looked down the steps into the cellar - only to find that the floor was beginning to flood. If this had not happened all of the food that was stored there would have been ruined. The owners are quite happy with their visitor who seems to help and not hinder.

The name of **The Cat and Fiddle Inn**, **Hinton Admiral** may derive from Caton Le Fidelis, after the Knight Caton who faithfully held Calais against the French. The Inn was a haunt of smugglers bringing goods from the shores of Christchurch Bay at Chewton Bunny, Avon Beach and Mudeford Quay, for onward delivery to the Queens Head at Burley and the smugglers market at Ridley Wood in the depths of the New Forest. The oldest part of the building was supposed to be haunted, footsteps and rattling noises heard when no one was there but since the inn has been renovated and turned into a restaurant reports of any ghostly activity seem to have ceased.

The Cat and Fiddle Inn, Hinton Admiral

Three Tuns Inn on the Ringwood Road at Bransgore, also an old building with possible smuggling connections, has a ghost associated with its barn on the south east side of the inn. A misty figure is said to emerge from the gate to St. Mary's Churchyard and cross the road diagonally to the barn at the Three Tuns.

A pretty cottage near the cross roads at **Bashley** is reported as being haunted; it was the site of a murder. It has been said that it is an unlucky residence and that partly due to its atmosphere occupants are at risk of marital discord.

Cox's Bridge at Milford-on-Sea is said to be haunted by a headless small boy who sits on the parapet of the bridge.

Lymington

Angel Inn in Lymington High Street, an old coaching inn, was formerly called St. George and Dragon. It is said to have three ghosts: a coachman who has been seen standing by the kitchen windows looking out when dawn is breaking; a young girl, perhaps a maid or a child with long fair hair, in a white dress who has been seen on the second floor, and a tall mariner with grey hair and a naval coat buttoned to the neck. There are also reports of a ghostly piano being played, when there was no such instrument on the premises.

Stanwell House Hotel, also in Lymington High Street, was once a young ladies finishing school. A room on the third floor is haunted by a young girl. A maid suddenly saw the child in the room when she was making the bed. The maid fled and would not return to the room.

Another haunted place in Lymington is **Bywater House**, formerly Formosa House. Here doors open and close for no apparent reason and animals have shown signs of fear. Noises like rolling casks and footsteps heard are said to be those of ghostly smugglers. Other noises have been attributed to the unquiet spirit of a murdered courier acting for the Duke of Monmouth. Perhaps he was seeking a vessel for his master's escape. The Duke was captured near Ringwood and executed at London by order of his uncle James II.

East of the mouth of the Lymington River **Pylewell Home Farm** is supposed to be haunted by the ghosts of smugglers. Noises akin to barrels being rolled on the floor have been heard in the upper rooms of the house.

The church at **Boldre** is supposed to be haunted by two medieval archers who have been seen kneeling at the altar.

Hurn

Parley Lane, Hurn from Merritown Farm

In 1988 a figure in RAF uniform was seen riding a bicycle along Parley Lane at **Merritown Farm**, opposite the Alice and Wonderland maze near Hurn Airport. The figure was nearly run down by a car, but the figure and bike dematerialised. Hurn Airport was opened in October 1940 as an RAF Station.

Prior to the Second World War the smokehouse of a farm in **East Parley** emitted an overwhelming feeling of misery and despair. It appears that during the 1840's, a time of considerable poverty and mass starvation throughout England, a child had broken into the smokehouse through the roof to steal some bacon, but was caught by his clothing on a hook used for hanging bacon and suffocated in the fumes of the smokehouse.

Gibbit Firs, Parley Common, on the former county boundary of Dorset and Hampshire was the site of a gibbet where two men were hung for the murder of the father of one of them. The murdered man's widow went mad and tried to feed the corpses of the men suspended in the iron gibbets. The gibbet post was eventually cut down to deprive grisly relic hunters. The stump of the post is now the base of the sundial in West Parley Churchyard. However no ghosts have been reported here!

Bournemouth

Hengistbury Head has a ghostly horseman seen on at least three occasions in the 1980's. The name of Hengistbury Head was not recorded until Victorian times when ancient earthworks (such as Double Dykes) were often linked to historical characters (Hengist and Horsa).

Hengistbury Head from the air looking west

The earliest known reference is an undated charter of Baldwin de Redvers calling it Hednesburia. It may relate to 'stone horse fort' or 'stallion fort' or, 'seafoam horse fort'. Such a horseman could be one of several historical figures: a customs Riding Officer; a dragoon or RHA gunner from Christchurch Barracks (1794-1994); a Radknight (messenger) of which Domesday records four at Christchurch; a hobler (light horseman) manning the Hengistbury Head shore line triple beacon of Tudor and Napoleonic times. Hoblers get their name from carrying a hobble for their horses, which could thus be left to graze but not stray. The Hengistbury beacon linked with other shore beacons: to the west at Lansdowne and beyond to Canford Cliffs, to the east to Hordle and to the Isle of Wight, inland to the coast hill double beacon at St. Catherine's Hill.

In **Bournemouth Pleasure Gardens** a figure in a black hooded cloak with a nun's cowl has been seen in Invalids Walk at night. The figure is frightening and is also said to have a non-human face.

Bournemouth Town Hall was formerly a hospital and a female figure in long dress has been seen in corridor when it was not in use.

The premises of **2CR** in Southcote Road are supposedly haunted. A presenter of one of the radio programmes working alone in the studio one night saw a reflection of a well-built man in the glass but there was no one there. On another occasion a caretaker, also alone, heard the shutters on a window rattling and shaking from the corridor outside. As he entered the room the noise stopped and the shutter was still. He checked that the window was closed – which it was. As he left the room the shutter started rattling and shaking again.

A dog haunted a family house in the **Holdenhurst Road**. In 1968 the fiancée of the son of the house was staying the night. The next day she reported that she had seen the family's pet collie dog in her bedroom. However the dog had been in a traffic accident and died while at the vets on the evening of her visit, but she was unaware of this.

King's Park Hospital, Boscombe, is based on an administration building, which was once a sanatorium. The first floor is supposed to be haunted by a female figure wearing Victorian clothes.

Hamilton Road Orphanage, Boscombe, is now a block of flats. There have been reports of hearing footsteps in one of the corridors and of 'uneasy' feelings there, possibly ghostly nuns checking on the orphans' dormitories.

Herbert House, Alumhurst Road

In Alumhurst Road, Westbourne, **Nightingale House**, part of Herbert Hospital, was built in about 1867 and possibly used as a soldiers' convalescent home after the Crimean War. During the 1970's Female staff reported a female figure in a long dark dress. It was suggested that the figure was Florence Nightingale who is also supposed to haunt the site of the military hospital at Netley. A similar story is told of a hotel at **Westcliff** in Bournemouth. Miss Nightingale is buried at East Wellow, southwest of Romsey, where there are also ghost stories concerning her.

Marler House, an office block at Westbourne, is built on the site of a doctor's house. The house is haunted by a tall male figure in a cloak, with a tall hat, which is thought to be the doctor.

A baker used to haunt a locked and empty Westbourne building, which has since been demolished, next to the **Westbourne** Hotel. Apparently an ugly old man's face was seen at a window on several occasions and the window was opened and closed, as with footsteps and drops in temperature, reports of faces at windows are relatively common. After one sighting the building was quickly unlocked and the room checked but it was quite empty. However the windowsill was covered in a layer of white dust like flour but there were no fingerprints on either the sill or the window catch.

Another empty house was the cause of concern. A plumber working alone in the **Bournemouth** property was aware of a depressive atmosphere and his radio lost power. He was conscious of an icy coldness and could feel a presence in the room but couldn't see anything. Gradually the atmosphere lightened, the room lost its icy feel and the radio worked normally.

At **Wimborne Road** in Kinson the sound of horses have been heard but nothing seen.

A figure of a youth in a white raincoat haunts **DeCoy Pond Park,** where a council workman was murdered with his own scythe. The ghost is the murderer, who in later life was termed a lunatic, and who returns to the scene of the crime.

Outside premises in **Poole Road**, Bournemouth, a headless, male figure in a dark uniform has been seen on the pavement in the early hours of the morning. On one night several different people saw the figure over the course of a few hours. He is thought to have been a guillotined French soldier although the guillotine was never used in England.

At **Webster Road** in Bournemouth in the 1970's, a newly married couple were woken by noises down stairs. On investigating the empty room, which had shut doors and windows, there was a movement in the curtains and the sense of someone or something leaving the room.

An unusual story is reported by a Bournemouth family named Burden. They were haunted by the ghost of a teenage boy who had fallen in love with family's 17-year-old daughter. On an August morning in 1981 at their home in **Abbott Road**, Winton, Mrs Burden was at home with her foster son Bradley, a mentally retarded 8 year old, when ornaments and crockery started flying around the room and crashing to the floor. Mrs Burden called for help and her husband came home immediately. He was aware of a strange and icy atmosphere pervading the house. The poltergeist activity continued and a priest was summoned to exorcise the house.

The following day the poltergeist activity continued and only stopped when Bradley and his mother left the house. Later that day a séance was held in the house and the daughter was 'taken over' by a troubled spirit called Ian. He was one of Debbie's friends, a drug addict who had since died. Ian was also Bradley's imaginary friend who used to get him to do naughty things. Ian had come through Bradley, as being retarded he apparently provided an open and therefore easy channel. He showed himself to Bradley as a boy although he was a young man when he died.

Further Ghosts Stories From the Surrounding Area

Poole

An old woman in grey and wearing an apron has been seen walking across the courtyard of **Scalpens Court** and up the stairs. This is possibly the ghost of Agnes Beard, a maidservant, who with her mistress, Alice Green, was murdered by burglars in 1598.

High Street, Poole

In 1965 and 1966 objects were seen moving, as if in slow motion, in a shop in the **High Street**. On other occasions items on shelves in another High Street shop have been thrown to the ground. Over the years there have been many reported sightings of ghosts in various High Street premises including a man who is known as 'Jenkins' in evening dress seen standing on a flight of stairs.

From an old building in **Market Street** there were noises like heavy furniture being moved, banging on the floor and noisy footsteps were heard. The room from which the noises emanated was found disordered though there was no sign of a break-in; water was found on chairs and icy hands could be felt although there was no one in the room.

In the **Crown Hotel**, Market Street, the sound of piano playing was heard coming from a room with no piano. Other instances of hauntings at this hotel include the noise of footsteps and of casks being rolled, a door seen to shut and open of its own accord and a fluorescent mist on the stairs seen to move down and out of the hotel and across the courtyard.

Byngley House, also in Market Street, has a bedroom with a suffocating atmosphere. In the 16th century Thomas White who was a Mayor of Poole on several occasions owned the house. He was a wealthy man and a 'Papist'. The room may once have held a 'Papist' domestic chapel.

In the **Guildhall**, Market Street, footsteps have been heard when the building was empty. It has been suggested they belonged to a nineteenth century clerk who committed suicide.

When two cottages in **New Street** were subject to building work to convert them into one property, footsteps were heard in an empty room. This room also had a cold atmosphere.

Whilst modernising a Georgian style house at the corner of **New Street** and **Cinnamon Lane** in 1973 a builder saw a male figure with long hair and wearing a long greenish coat suddenly appear in an upstairs room.

King Charles Inn is another haunted pub in Poole Old Town. In 1984 there were reports of many strange happenings here. Apart from footsteps being heard in various parts of the pub late at night with no obvious explanation, items such as a wedding dress had gone missing, the games machine frequently malfunctioned and the pub dog refused to go into some of the rooms.

St Anne's Hospital, Canford Cliffs, was built about 1910 and was once a sanatorium. Ghostly figures in old-fashioned clothing have been seen in the gardens. The area was once much frequented by smugglers using local chines. There was also a shoreline beacon in the area, which was on a Roman signal route from St Catherine's Hill to Corfe and also on a Tudor one from Beacon Hill to Lansdowne.

A cottage in **Dunford Road**, Parkstone was haunted by the dead grandparents of the resident family who saw and identified the ghosts. The family noticed that objects had been moved, they heard noises and smelt beer and tobacco; the sounds and smells associated with the grandparents. The cottage was alleged to have once been used by smugglers.

A daughter of the same family lived nearby at **Runton Road** and she also reported hauntings by the deceased relatives: the sound of her deceased grandfather's scissors, he had been a barber, and the smell of violets. Her baby in its pram could apparently see something and would chuckle and stretch out arms to someone not visible to others. A three-year-old member of the family spoke to his grandfather who was dead but the child was unaware of this at the time.

An early 19th century cottage known as **Mount Talbot** stood on what is now Sainsbury's Supermarket at Alder Hills, Parkstone. Strange people reputedly haunted the cottage and weird noises were apparently heard at night. The cottage may well have been used to house contraband as it was on a smugglers route from Canford Cliffs to Kinson.

Yarrells Lane in Upton has a house where a female figure has been seen coming up the drive but there is never anyone there.

An old house at **Hamworthy** has a garden haunted by the ghost of a gardener. The elderly gentleman sits on a seat, gazing at the garden before he fades from view.

A husband at **Hamworthy** shot his cousin when he discovered that he was his wife's lover. The man's body was thrown into a pond. The ghost is supposed to whistle to call out his lover from the house.

In the reign of Edward VI a ship carrying 8 bells sunk during a storm just outside Poole Harbour, near **Old Harry Rocks**, and all the crew were drowned. It is said that the eerie cries of the crew and the peal of the bells can be heard at night as a warning to passing sailors.

The Old Harry Rocks

A ghostly funeral procession has been witnessed on the Poole to **Lytchett Minster** road. The 4 headless coffin bearers walked into a hedge whereupon they disappeared.

Whispering voices have been heard near a field path at **Lytchett Matravers**. A female figure in old-fashioned black clothes has been seen in the church, a sigh heard and icy breath felt but no one was there.

At the **Manor House** in Lytchett Matravers, a candle seen from outside the house was apparently being carried from room to room but no one was there. A similar tale is told of a cottage near Wimborne.

Wimborne

A pretty girl in her mid teens haunts a property in **Riverside Mews**, Mill Lane. The ghost is 'Annie', a girl who had been raped and murdered by the miller. She is mischievous and speaks, moves furniture and other objects, breaks plates and turns on and off electrical equipment. Hand bells have also been heard. Some people feel they are being watched and although one person has experienced feelings of dread, most people are not intimidated by her presence. Animals have been known to react to a particular site on the wall here where there used to be a door.

At the **Pudding and Pye Inn**, Wimborne, a knocking has been heard at the door and a voice softly calling the landlady's name when there was no one there.

A grey nun has been seen crossing the road near the **Old Grammar School** at Wimborne.

A headless horse accompanied by a headless man has been seen on a hill near **Rowlands** at Wimborne.

The ghost that haunts the **Kings House**, West Borough, is a clergyman, thought to be the Rev. Percy Newell who lived at the house from 1843. An owner of the house had seen him walking into the drawing room on the ground floor through a wall where there had once been a door into the adjoining property. During the Second World War a visitor reported seeing the figure of a clergyman dressed in black and carrying a bible walking through a wall into the adjoining house. In 2002 a tall thin man wearing a dog collar and hat of a clergyman from an earlier era was seen in the early hours of the morning standing in a bedroom close to the bed and staring down at the husband while he slept. The wife asked him to leave her husband alone and he faded from her sight.

At the crossroads between **Colehill** and **Hinton Park**, a ghostly coffin has been seen in the middle of the road near a barn that was the site of a suicide. People who took their own lives were not allowed to be buried in consecrated ground. The road here is in no man's land between the two parishes.

In 1927 at **Bottlebush Down**, near Squirrel's Corner on B3081 road towards Handley Cross, an archaeologist on his way home from Christchurch saw a Bronze Age horseman 50 yards from the road. The two men looked at each other and the horseman travelled parallel with the car brandishing a weapon until he vanished with his horse into a round barrow. Other people have been similarly followed and frightened by this ancient ghost.

The **B3082 road** from Blandford to Wimborne has ghostly horses. There was a Leper Hospital on this road about a mile out of Wimborne. The road passes the large Iron Age hill fort of Badbury Rings where there was also a Roman temple.

In 1972 in **Millham's Lane**, Longham, a grey figure in a cape was seen on the road in the early morning.

The River Stour

A lady in a long white dress and a bonnet has been seen at various times along the banks of the River Stour between **Longham** and **Kinson**. The Bournemouth Echo reported that she had been seen in 1971 by a boy at Longham near the Bridge House Hotel and also on another occasion by a man working in his back garden at Longham. The ghost is of similar appearance to one previously seen haunting a cottage in Wimborne Road near Bear Cross prior to it being pulled down. Perhaps she is now homeless.

Between **Longham Bridge** and Bridge House Hotel a male figure in a long mackintosh has been seen on an old fashioned bicycle, riding without lights and on wrong side of road. He was seen at 9.35pm on 11th April 1994 when a car drove right through the figure, but no one was there.

At the pub **The Old Thatch** at Uddens, Ferndown, there have been reports of chairs falling over and kitchen utensils flying about. The premises are alleged to be the site of the death of an old lady in a rocking chair and also of a former pub manager who died after falling downstairs.

A ruined medieval church is situated in the centre of one of three Neolithic henges at **Knowlton**. The site is often visited at sunrise and sunset during solstices and other festivals. It is alleged that there have been strange noises and feelings of cold and some people have experienced sensations of fear. The village, which the church served, was wiped out the Black Death. The site has a reputation of witchcraft. At least 18 ley lines go through Church Henge at Knowlton.

Bone Acre Copse, Wimborne St Giles, is haunted by a hooded female figure and by the sound of a wagon and horses at speed.

A bungalow at **Hampreston** near Ferndown is on a reputed smugglers' route and in 1969 was haunted by slow footsteps and doors opening and closing on their own.

Ringwood

In 1941 a monk-like figure was seen by children near a house in **Salisbury Road**, **Bisterne** (the road from Christchurch to Ringwood). The figure was seen again in 1995.

Female staff and also a child saw a lovely woman in a flowing crinoline dress at the **White Hart Inn** in the Market Place at Ringwood.

The former **Four Seasons Restaurant** at the Market Place was haunted by a woman in a long grey dress. She was believed to be a former resident who was killed in a traffic accident. Cutlery and crockery moved about or were broken and patches of coldness were experienced. A young visitor to the premises was so startled to see an old lady in grey sitting in a chair at the top of a flight of stairs that he fell back down the stairs knocking himself out.

As with many old coaching inns in the area people have reported hearing footsteps at the **Crown Inn** in Southampton Road, Ringwood when there has been no one there. A female figure in long dress has been seen in a corridor and on another occasion a man staying at the hotel reported that a lady with grey hair had gently touched his face and walked round the room before she suddenly disappeared. Earlier this year a guest was surprised to find that a grey haired lady wearing a grey dress was waiting outside his room holding a towel. He was even more surprised when he was told that no one else was booked into the hotel at the time. Members of staff have been aware of a 'coldness' and a feeling of being watched but think that the ghost is friendly. At the Crown Tap next door one of the staff saw a ghost of young boy wearing a vest and khaki shorts who just stared at him. He thought it was his son who was fast asleep upstairs.

The Cottage, an adjoining building in Southampton Road, also has a ghost. Noises have been heard outside a first floor bedroom, a dress rustling, curtains moving and a door handle that turns when no one is there. Occupants have the impression that the ghost is kindly and wants to look after them.

Opposite the **Granary**, Ringwood, near the site of a former slaughterhouse, horses hooves have been heard when none were present.

In 1967 children saw a man and a woman dressed in Georgian clothes at a cottage in **Ebenezer Lane**, Ringwood. The ghosts were not visible to adults.

Candlesticks, a restaurant in Christchurch Road, Ringwood, was originally 3 old cottages. In medieval times the middle cottage was owned by a midwife who would put a burning candle in the window of her cottage to show when she was at home and could be contacted. There have been reports of crockery and ornaments being moved in the restaurant when no one has been there and a waitress saw a spoon fly off the table and land on the floor. Customers have commented on a new waitress, who didn't exist. When asked about her they have described a lady in a long white calico dress and apron and with a mobcap on her head, which could be the dress of a medieval midwife. When the ghost is around an aroma of an old-fashioned fragrance similar to lavender or lily of the valley wafts around the building.

The ghost of a Cavalier has also been seen at Candlesticks. He walked through the wall where there used to be a door before the front wall of the restaurant was renovated. During the English Civil War the building was apparently used as a billet for an officer. At the back of the building near the garage is an old wall with hitching rings for horses. Many people have reported hearing horses here when there have been none around. When the present owners moved in 20 years ago they had the roof re-thatched and employed an old family firm of thatchers to do the job. An elderly relative of the workers recalled a time when his grandfather worked on the roof and found a complete Cromwellian uniform hidden in the loft.

A female figure with a shawl covering her head has been seen passing through a hedge at **Horton Heath**.

A woman in an old fashioned dress haunts the **High Corner Inn, Linwood**.

Moyles Court, a 17th century house and now a school was once the home of Dame Alice Lisle, the widow of a regicide. Dame Alice was sentenced to death for sheltering fugitives from Monmouth's rebellion in 1685. Judge Jeffreys originally sentenced her to burning but due to public revulsion the sentence was mitigated to decapitation. In 1962 Dame Alice appeared in the house as a solid person in a black dress and spoke to visitors who thought she was a guide. She has been seen, with her head under her arm, walking around the house and surrounding area; and also whilst travelling from Ellingham Church to Moyles Court, in a coach drawn by headless horses and no coachman. People have been aware of the sudden smell of violets at Moyles Court.

People camping at the old museum and the car park at **Rockborne Roman Villa** near Fordingbridge, north of Ringwood, have reported intense feelings of fear and an evil atmosphere, like a mist, hanging over them at night. The noise of cartwheels has also been heard.

Beaulieu and the New Forest

Beaulieu Abbey was once a monastery. Chanting Cistercian white monks and labouring brown monks have been heard and seen. Instances of ghostly activities include smells associated with the monks, loss of balance and cold patches. Isabella, wife of 2nd Duke, haunts the Palace House cottages and gardens, once part of the Abbey, wearing a blue dress. Phantom dogs and doppelgangers have also been reported at different times.

During World War II the Special Operations Executive trained agents at **Beaulieu**. Trainees reported seeing brown habit monks, as did two artillery officers and various civilians. White habit monks were seen by some boys in 1957.

Palace House, Beaulieu

In the **New Forest** a cyclist was overcome by fear and had a feeling of great weight pressing down on him. On a separate occasion two men walking in the forest in fog were overtaken by horses, riders and hounds that passed over them. Two other travellers on a moon lit night were three times passed by the same figure of a large man which walked towards them dressed in Georgian clothes.

A small, weeping boy running along the track, haunts the footpath at **Picket Post** near Burley. The child was alleged to have been drowned by a Burley couple because they could not afford to feed him.

At the **Queen's Head Inn**, Burley, once a smuggling inn, ghostly noises, alleged to be smugglers have been heard. Renovations uncovered an unknown cellar believed to be a hiding place of the smugglers as it contained pistols, bottles and coins.

The Queens Head Inn, Burley

Burley is well known for its association with witches and has a gift shop called 'The Coven of Witches'. Sybil Leek, a white witch, lived in the village during the 1950's and dressed in her long black cloak was often seen walking around with her pet jackdaw on her shoulder.

A ghostly procession passes across the car park of the **Hare and Hounds Inn, Sway**, on the way to a gibbet at Marlpit Oak. In 2001 pictures on the wall on the first floor of the pub and books on shelves were moved or thrown on the floor.

Fox and Hounds Inn, Lyndhurst, is haunted by a male ghost, possibly a former landlord.

Northeast of Lyndhurst towards **Ashurst**, the ghosts of a murdered woman and her child were seen which enabled their remains to be discovered nearly forty years later. The suspected murderer then committed suicide.

The Filly Inn, Setley, near Brockenhurst, is haunted by one of three highwaymen who were hung for murder and who was later repentant for this evil deed. The highwaymen ambushed and murdered a traveller returning to the inn suspecting that he was carrying a large sum of money. Having stolen his money and thrown his body in the pool at Latchmore the three called at an inn at Setley where they drank greedily and bragged about their deed. They were duly caught and hanged at Marlpit Oak and the inn became known locally as the 'Three Murderers'. To rid the inn of its bad reputation it has since been pulled down and rebuilt.

A lady in white haunts the **churchyard at Exton**, at the mouth of River Otter, which is also known as Beaulieu River.

The **New Forest** brought ill luck to the Conqueror's family: one son and grandson were killed at different times by tree branches when galloping through the forest. A shaft from a hunting crossbow in the forest killed another son, William II – Rufus the Red. William Rufus was a cruel and unpopular king who offended the church, the nobility and the common people. He ignored his promises to cut taxes and institute better government and he held church appointments vacant in order to appropriate their revenues. He was probably murdered, for many people at all levels of society hated him, and many stood to gain by his removal including his younger brother Henry.

A member of the hunting party, Gerald of Wales, stated much later that the killer was Ranulf de Aquis. It is possible that this was the former Dean of the Holy Trinity (later Priory) at Christchurch,

Ranulf Flambard, Bishop of Durham, who was also part of the hunting party, along with Sir Walter Tyrrell whom is usually blamed. When he was near to his death Tyrrell told Abbot Sugar that he was not the killer.

The Rufus Stone, New Forest

Immediately after the fatal wounding occurred Tyrrell left for France to tell of the news, probably taking a ship from Christchurch or from North Shore at Poole. Tyrrell was given the blame for the death as due to an accident – the shaft allegedly having glanced off a tree but no action was ever taken against him. Rumour has it that his ghost has been seen on his horse riding down **Tyrrell Lane**.

Other Strange Events

A case of human combustion at Christchurch was reported at Christchurch in June 1613. Details have been reported in several books including: *Human Combustion* by Randers and Hough, *Spontaneous Combustion* by D. Wilson and *Fire from Heaven* by Rev. John Hilliard, a local clergyman, whose pamphlet recounts the following story.

A carpenter at Christchurch, named John Hitchen, was found dead in bed by his mother-in-law. Also in the bed were his wife and child, the latter died but Mrs Hitchen survived with burns. Hitchen's corpse was on fire and continued to smoulder for three days after it was dragged out of the house.

Hitchen's mother-in-law, Mrs Russel, slept in the same room and had been woken up by what felt to be a violent blow to her cheek. She called for help but could not be heard due to a violent thunderstorm raging at the time. She went to her son-in-law and daughter's bed that was surrounded by smoke. She woke her daughter who despite burns was deeply asleep.

John Hitchen's corpse was very hot and burned from the inside (this is typical in human combustion cases). Smoke poured from his body but there was no external flame.

Such cases may be due to electro-magnetic phenomena interacting in certain circumstances with cells in the human body and burning chemicals (like phosphorous) and gasses (like methane) within the body. In such cases the body burns like a candle and consumes itself but often does not ignite other objects. Frequently the extremities of the arms and legs are left unburnt.

If electro-magnetic energy is associated with ley lines it may be significant that several leylines pass through Christchurch, with some focusing on the Priory site. Others focus at St. Catherines Hill chapel site, Hengistbury Head, the site of Holdenhurst Long Barrow, and the suspected site of the long barrow at North Bockhampton.

In 1921 a young cook from London was tricked into travelling to Bournemouth after receiving a bogus telegram sent from Boscombe Post Office. She was found murdered on heath land the following day. Months passed and the police had made little progress in tracing her killer. After an appeal to the public for help a local spiritualist gave the police a detailed description of the murderer. The murderer was soon caught and convicted the following year.

In October 1978 a small aircraft set off from Hurn Airport en route to Alderney. About 25 miles out over the Channel the instruments went wild. The compass direction indicator spun 100° in clockwise direction. The pilot had to take navigation fixes by radio direction finder; 12 minutes later all returned to normal. On the return trip the same thing occurred but the deviation was only 20°. This strange event thus appeared to have declined in force. It may have been due to some electro-magnetic pulse, or perhaps military tests of some kind.

In 1981 there was a fall of small yellow frogs at Bournemouth, during a thunderstorm. This could have occurred due to a whirlwind updraft lifting them into the air until they later fell to earth.

On 5th June 1983 pieces of coke, some over two inches in diameter fell in a thunderstorm over a wide area of Poole, Bournemouth and Christchurch. This was also probably due to whirlwinds.

In the summer of 1984 little balls of damp sand fell on numerous occasions at Tuckton. It is not uncommon for sand to be found on car windscreens, deposited in rain having been sucked into the upper air by winds over North Africa.

A mysterious hum has often been heard in Poole, Bournemouth, Christchurch and elsewhere and no suitable explanation has been found.

Booms and bangs have been heard frequently. They are often due to artillery practice at sea or on the Isle of Purbeck. Some have also been attributed to Concorde or other sonic bangs due to aircraft. Some may have been seismic or atmospheric.

In October 1969 a glowing object, five inches in diameter, was seen on a hotel veranda in Bournemouth. It flew out to sea. It may have been a form of ball lightening.

In the 1980's and again in 2002, unidentified flying objects were reported over Hengistbury Head. The apparent size, speed and manoeuvrability of these objects made them difficult to identify as conventional aircraft.

Reports of Strange Animals

In the medieval period the cathedral at Laon in France burnt down and monks from that city travelled widely to raise funds for its reconstruction. They came to Christchurch but received no help since the Priory was still under construction. The Laon monks were turned out of town and so they put a curse on Christchurch that a sea monster would come to harm the place. A similar curse was placed on Bodmin and other towns where they received an ill reception. A five-headed monster is supposed to have come from the sea and devastated Christchurch. This could be based on five fires in the thatched town, perhaps started by sea-borne pirates. Accidental fires were also common.

Such a monster may have given rise to the story of a dragon at Castle Hill in Burley, overlooking the River Avon. The dragon made daily visits to Bisterne much to the villagers' annoyance. Legend has it that the local lord of the manor, Sir Maurice de Berkley, a knight in shining armour, slew the dragon for the people. To celebrate the story a carving of a dragon was placed over the entrance to Bisterne Manor and nearby is a road called Dragon Lane.

A dead whale or a giant squid could have been regarded in years gone by as a sea monster if it was found washed up on the beach. Similarly it could have been a living seal or other sea creature that had penetrated inland by swimming up a river.

In July 1958 a monster was spotted in the sea 200 yards off Avon Beach from a Tiger Moth aeroplane flying over the area. Local newspapers reported several more sightings of the monster over the summer. The consensus of opinion was that it was probably a basking shark.

A seal was seen in the River Stour in 2001 and came ashore into private gardens at Tuckton.

In the late 1970's a crocodile was at large in the Stour at Iford for five summer months. It had escaped from a circus and supported itself on fish until it was recaptured.

At different times various unusual birds have been seen in the area: pelicans and flamingos have been seen in Christchurch Harbour and a peacock in the author's garden at Highcliffe in 2000. These birds have probably been blown off course from Africa or escaped from private collections.

Misericord with Green Man, Christchurch Priory

Some Conclusions

Ghostly happenings trigger one or more of our senses and many "hauntings" involve some kind of noise. Hence there are likely to be natural explanations for some of the reports such as building settlement, noise from winds, the temperature effects on wood, plastic or metal, even the movement of insects or rodents. Visual reports may, in some cases, be due to the effects of light and shadow. Not all ghostly effects can be easily explained away as having natural causes though. There are still many questions left unanswered for example: Why can some people see ghosts where others cannot? How are ghosts witnessed by children but not by accompanying adults? Why can people see ghosts in some places but not in others that are known to be haunted? Why are there not more ghosts from ancient times? Why are the reports of ghosts of animals confined to those with a close association with humans such as horses and dogs?

There seems to be a high correlation between ghosts and suicides. Is it because people who had taken their own lives had committed a criminal offence in English law (repealed in 1961) and were once denied a proper burial? Until the 1820's the burial of suicides was carried out at night in unconsecrated ground, often at cross roads, without a burial service and often with a stake driven through the heart.

The opinions and experiences of readers are of interest. Please write down your observations of unusual events and send them to me Michael A. Hodges c/o Natula Publications, 5 St Margarets Avenue, Christchurch. BH23 1JD. So many people have a ghostly experience but fail to pass it on for fear of embarrassment. Such experiences are for more common than we suppose and by sharing them we can try better to understand them.

There may be a tendency for ghostly events to appear on ley lines, which could be associated with electromagnetic energy. Accurate record keeping of events can aid the understanding of things only labelled as supernatural because we currently lack knowledge.

An ancient road in the New Forest

About the Author

Michael A. Hodges, M.A. FCIPD, MCIM is a retired personnel manager for a leading British financial institution who has also been a management consultant, a Customs and Excise and NBPI investigator, and a regular soldier. He has been Christchurch Mayor, councillor and local school governor and is currently Governor of Brockenhurst Further Education College.

Michael actively promotes archaeology and local history in Christchurch and has chaired various committees in these fields including Christchurch Local History Society, and The Friends of the Red House Museum. He has also been a member of the Dorset Archaeological Committee and the Christchurch Town Centre Forum Steering Committee. Michael's other interests include the Dorset Earth Mysteries Group, and the Ley Hunters Society of which he is the present Chairman.

He has written some dozen publications, many dealing with aspects of local history, including: -

Prepared for Battle, forts and fights in and near Christchurch over three millennia, 1982.
Helis the Cerne Giant and links with Christchurch, 1998.
The Smuggler: No Gentleman, smuggling with violence around Christchurch and Poole Bays; Natula Publications, 1999.
Christchurch in World War II (Part 1), coastal defences, anti tank island, civil defence; CLHS, 2001.
Christchurch in World War II (Part 2), secret war, ROC, airfields, the sea; CHLS, 2001.
Christchurch, a photographic history of your town; Black Horse Books for W.H. Smith, 2001.

BIBLIOGRAPHY

R. Boar and N. Blundell, **The World's Greatest Ghosts**, Hamlyn, 1991.

J. & C. Bord, **Modern Mysteries of Britain**, Diamond Books, 1991.

Bournemouth Daily Echo.

Christchurch Times.

I. Fox, **The Haunted Places of Hampshire,** Countryside Books, 1997.

R. Guttridge, **Ten Dorset Mysteries,** Ensign Publications 1989.

R. Legg, **Mysterious Dorset,** Dorset Publishing, 1987.

R. Long, **Haunted Inns of Hampshire**, Power Publications, 1999.

G. Osborn, **Dorset Curiosities**, Dovecote Press, 1986.

P. Ross, **Hampshire Hauntings and Hearsay**,
The King England Press, 1998.

J. Stubbs, **Dorset Mysteries**, Bossiney Books, 1989.

P. Underwood, **Ghosts of Hampshire and the Isle of Wight**,
St Michael's Abbey Press, 1983.

P. Underwood, **Mysterious Places**, Bossiney Books, Bodmin, 1988.

P. Underwood, **Ghosts of Dorset**, Bossiney Books, 1988.

E. Waring, **Ghosts and Legends of the Dorset Countryside**,
Compton Press, 1977.

P.M. Wilnecker, **Ghostly Tales of Wessex**, Poole, 1995.

D. Wilson, **Spontaneous Combustion**, Robinson Publishing, 1997.

Women's Institutes of Dorset, **Up Along Down Along**, 1935.